THE "ATLANTIC" 1832

"WINAN'S CAMEL" 1851

DIESEL ELECTRIC "51" 1937

With sincere gratitude to historian Sharon Harwood,
B&O Railroad employees past and present, and
Olive Dennis, Engineer Extraordinaire. – K.B.

For all the powerful women in the world. – T.S.

Library of Congress Control Number: 2022934872
ISBN 9781943147984

Text copyright © 2022 by Kaye Baillie
Illustrations by Tanja Stephani
Illustrations copyright © 2022 Tanja Stephani

Published by The Innovation Press
7511 Greenwood Avenue N. #4132, Seattle, WA 98103
www.theinnovationpress.com

Printed and bound by Worzalla
Production date March 2022

Cover art by Tanja Stephani
Book layout by Tim Martyn

RAILROAD ENGINEER

OLIVE DENNIS

WRITTEN BY
KAYE BAILLIE

ILLUSTRATED BY
TANJA STEPHANI

CUTTING
GLUING
CHECKING

Olive didn't just play with her dolls; she built them a whole house.
Two chimneys, two stories, and a clever arched door—perfect!

Olive loved to build things.

SAWING
HAMMERING
SANDING

As Olive grew, she spent more and more time in her father's workshop. With her very own toolset, she built a model streetcar for her brother, complete with a pivoting trolley pole and reversible seats.

Olive wished she could build things forever.

SHIFTING
LIFTING
LOWERING

After school, Olive rushed to watch the giant
derricks and cranes as they rattled and clunked.
When she asked a nearby workman questions,
he said he'd have to ask the engineer.

Her mind buzzing, Olive wondered what else engineers made.

In high school and college, Olive took classes in science, music, astronomy, and her favorite subject—math.

When her brother started studying civil engineering, Olive pored over his books, page after page, her mind racing!

Back then, people thought women were supposed to learn about

SEWING
COOKING
CLEANING

But Olive wondered, could she be an engineer? Slamming a book shut, she decided to find out.

$a^2 + b^2 = c^2$

Olive enrolled in civil engineering at Cornell University. When she walked into class, she felt odd being the only girl. But she wasn't about to let that worry her—she had roads, bridges, and buildings to design.

NOTES

She studied fluid dynamics

PUMPING
FLOODING
FLOWING

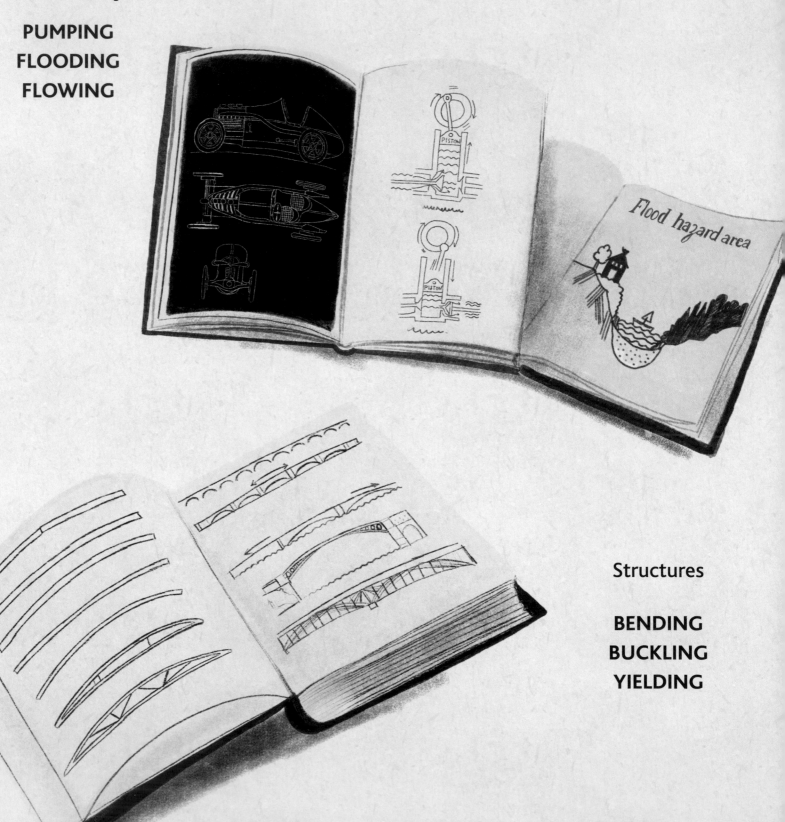

Structures

BENDING
BUCKLING
YIELDING

Transportation systems

**INTERSECTING
FUNCTIONING
MOVING**

Olive powered through the course in
one year, not two—with honors!
She couldn't wait to be an engineer.
But first, she needed a job.

At each place Olive applied, the men in charge
frowned and shook their heads. Even with a degree,
Olive knew they saw a woman—not a civil engineer.

Determined to succeed, Olive jumped
on a train back home to Baltimore.
There she found an ad.

APPLYING
HOPING
WAITING

This time, Olive got the job—as the first female engineer the B&O railroad ever employed.

RATING
CALCULATING
DESIGNING

Olive's main task during her first few months was to assess the railroad's old bridges and find ways to strengthen them. Soon after she was given a much more ambitious task—to design a deck girder bridge on her own!

When the president of the railroad called her into his office,
she wondered what exciting project was next.

But it wasn't what she expected.

The president told Olive that to increase business, they must encourage women to travel by train, not bus or car. In her new job as their first engineer of service, Olive would ride passenger trains and then suggest improvements—both as an engineer and as a woman.

Olive was used to working with a slide rule at a desk, not riding trains day in and day out. So, she agreed on one condition: if she didn't like the new job, she could return to the engineering department.

With that settled, Olive packed her
bags and climbed aboard the first B&O
train bound for anywhere.

**RIDING
TRYING
TESTING**

Olive soon realized there
was much she could do.

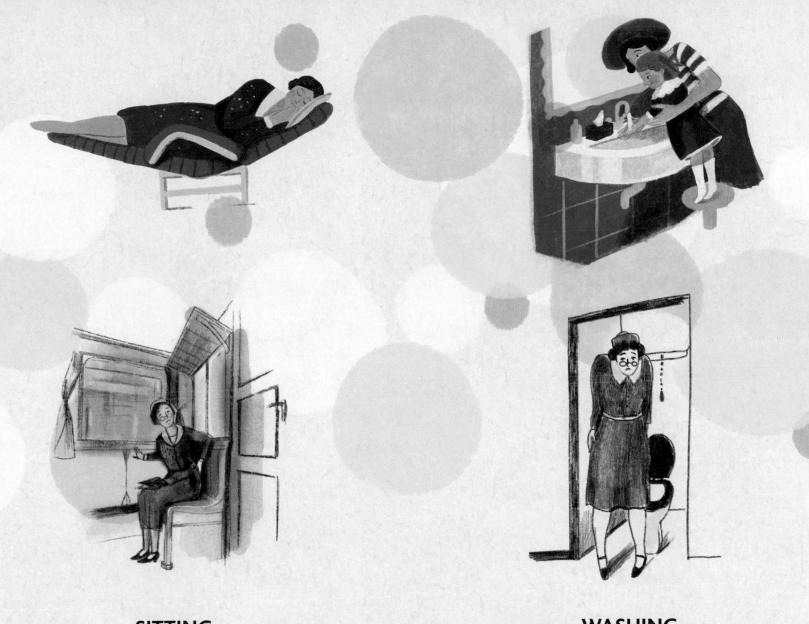

SITTING
ACHING

Olive recommended replacing
uncomfortable bench seats
with newly designed reclining
seats. She even figured out
how high the seats should be.
Not everyone had long legs!

WASHING
BUMPING

Olive suggested bigger
restrooms for moms and
babies—with actual doors.
A simple curtain would
not do!

**BREATHING
COUGHING**

Olive designed a window ventilator
to keep cinders out while letting fresh
air in. She detailed every spring, hinge,
plate, and pin!

**READING
SQUINTING**

Olive ordered dimmable ceiling
lights and introduced sidewall lamps.
Many passengers liked to read before
falling asleep!

WAITING
SWEATING

Olive found the insides of trains became hot while waiting at the station. She worked with a team to design the world's first fully air-conditioned train!

THINKING
FIXING

Ollve enjoyed finding and solving unique problems even if it meant tramping all day over the uneven terrain of cleaning and storage yards. Or sleeping on one kind of mattress while traveling to Chicago, then turning around and testing a different one on the ride home. Her notebook brimmed with ideas. Olive's improvements benefitted not just women, but all passengers on B&O trains.

One day, the president of the B&O
railroad called an urgent meeting. A rival
railroad boasted about their plans to build
a luxury daytime train that would be more
spacious, modern, and faster than any B&O
train—and within two years. Olive and her
team had made huge improvements, especially
to B&O's overnight trains, but to keep their
passengers and reputation, the B&O also
needed a luxury daytime train.

They needed an engineer to
design the outside.
They needed an engineer to
design the inside.
They needed one person . . .
Olive!

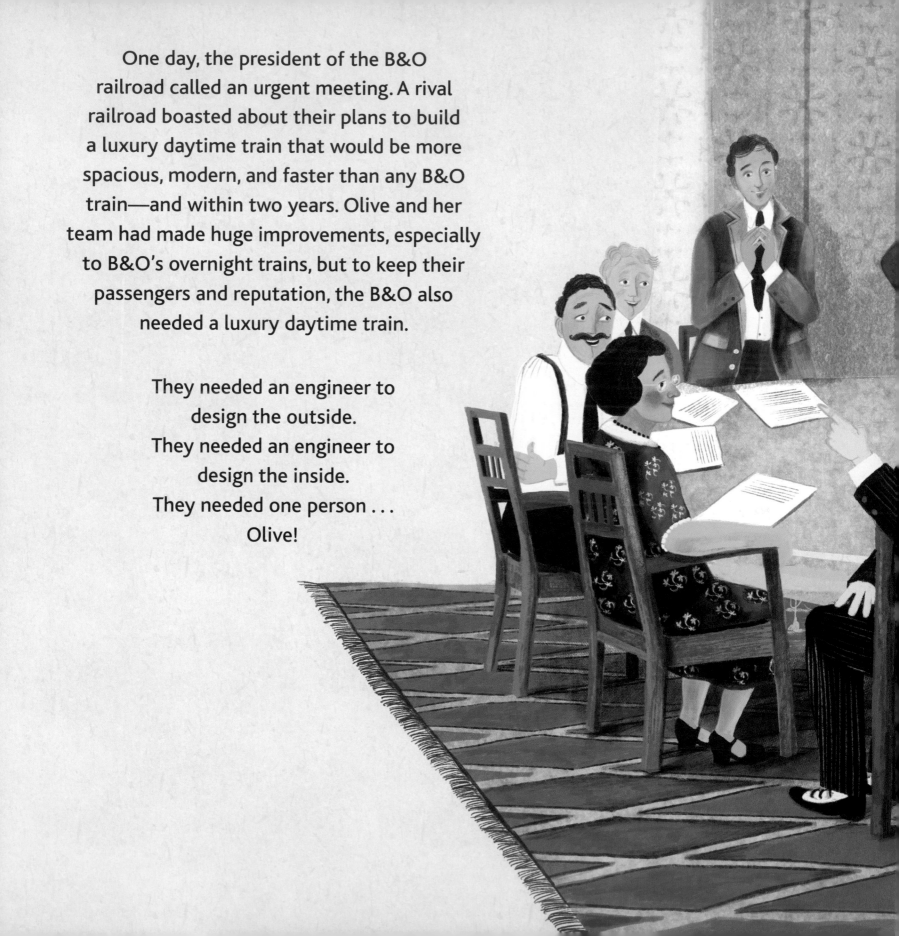

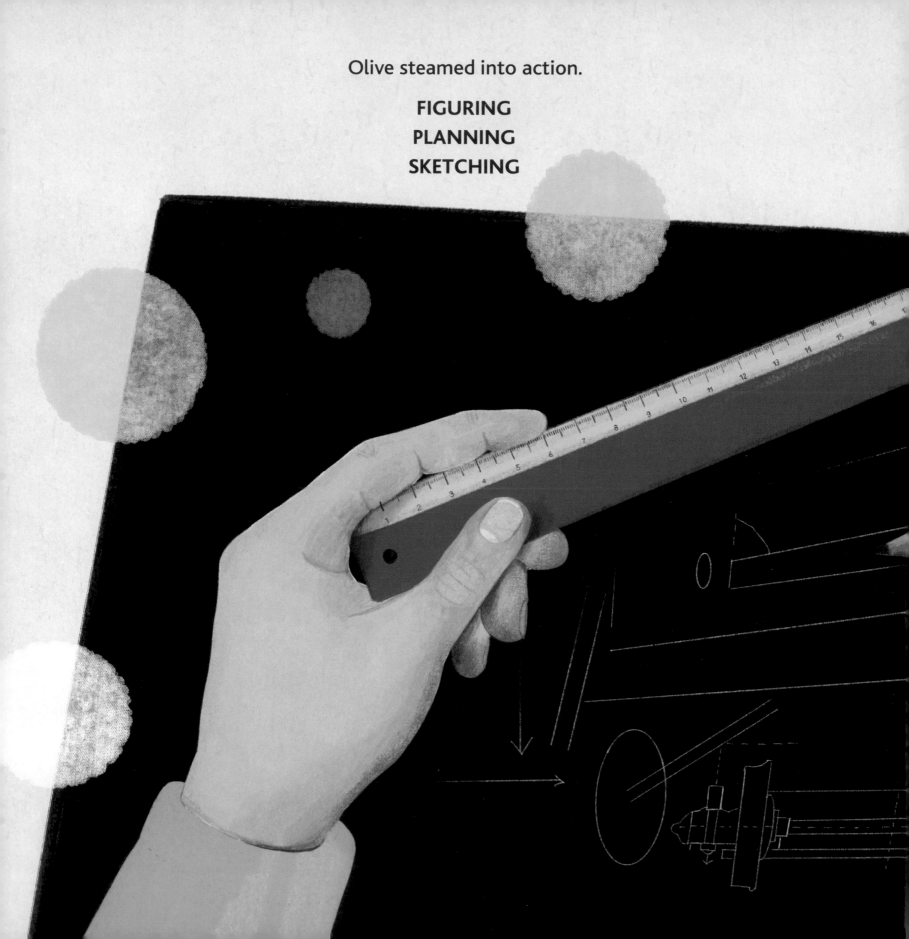

Olive steamed into action.

FIGURING
PLANNING
SKETCHING

To reduce stops, she redesigned the locomotives to carry more fuel and water. She restricted each train to five carriages to keep speed through the challenging Allegheny Mountains. She designed a slick, smooth engine cover, leaving room for fast repairs.

Once approved, Olive showed her team the new plans . . .
and they got to work.

CUTTING
SLOTTING
DRILLING

Bolting frames into place.

MELTING
POURING
CASTING

White-hot metal taking shape.

CLADDING
PAINTING
TRIMMING

Silver pinstripes decorating regal blue.

In just one year, not two, Olive and her team proudly presented—

SPARKLING
STEAMING
GLEAMING

THE CINCINNATIAN!

The first passengers climbed aboard . . .

RELAXING

Reclining seats with fresh new fabrics
of bold tans, sea greens, pretty blues,
and rose pinks.

REFRESHING

Spacious restrooms with mirrors,
medical kits, hot water, soap,
and paper towels.

INDULGING

A coffee shop car with lounge chairs
to make travelers feel at home.

GAZING

Windows with venetian blinds and
curtains instead of standard blinds.

SAVORING

A dining car with white tablecloths, silver coffee pots, and fancy plates. Even water carafes redesigned to fit hands of every size.

DELIGHTING

And at the back of the train, an observation lounge car with wraparound windows and rear-facing chairs so travelers could see where they'd been.

CHEERING

WHISTLING

BEAMING

Olive Dennis, railroad engineer.

Timeline

1885: Olive Dennis is born on November 20 in Thurlow, Pennsylvania.

1892: Relocates to Baltimore when her physician father moves the family. She builds a two-story wooden doll house complete with furniture.

1896: Builds a model streetcar for her little brother.

1904: Graduates as head of her class at Western High School. With a full scholarship, Olive enrolls at the Woman's College of Baltimore (now Goucher College).

1908: Graduates as a Phi Beta Kappa member from the Woman's College of Baltimore (now Goucher College). Receives an alumnae fellowship to attend Columbia University.

1909: Studies mathematics and astronomy, receiving a master of arts degree. Continues taking postgraduate courses at the University of Wisconsin engineering school. Begins a teaching career in mathematics at McKinley Manual Training School in Washington, DC.

1919: Enrolls as the only woman in her class at Cornell University's civil engineering program.

1920: Completes the civil engineering program in one year with honors, becoming the second woman to be awarded that degree from Cornell.

1920: Responds to an advertisement in the *Engineering News-Record* and gains a position as probationary bridge draftsman in the engineering department at Baltimore & Ohio Railroad. Becomes the first woman engineer employed by the railroad.

1921: Designs a deck girder bridge in Painesville, Ohio. As an engineer of service for B&O, she travels 44,000 miles of track in her first year on the job.

1923: Becomes the first female member of the American Railway Engineering Association.

1926: Designs the fleet of B&O motor buses.

1927: Files patent for the Dennis Ventilator.

1927: During bitter weather of January and February, identifies exact sites of twenty-three blockhouses erected along B&O lines during the Civil War used by federal troops guarding the bridges.

1930: After studying refrigerator cars in 1928, Olive works with mechanical personnel, resulting in B&O's first air-conditioned dining car, the Colonial Martha Washington. Designs the first rotating seats with reclining backs.

1931: The entire Columbian becomes the first completely air-conditioned train in world history.

1932: The National Limited becomes the first fully air-conditioned long-distance sleeping-car train in world history.

1938: Olive works with Otto Kuhler and his team on the 1938 heavyweight version of B&O's famous Royal Blue flagship train.

1940: Named one of the nation's 100 outstanding career women. President Roosevelt asks Olive to devise more efficient ways to move troops across the country during World War II.

1947: Olive designs the Cincinnatian one year ahead of schedule.

1949: Olive's streamlined Baldwin Cincinnatian is so successful, the design is sold to Indian State Railways for their Southern Railway.

1951: Olive Dennis retires.

1957: Olive Dennis dies age 71 in Baltimore, Maryland.

Bibliography and Suggested Reading

"Can A Woman Be A Civil Engineer?" *Baltimore and Ohio Magazine*, January 1921.

"Lady Railroad Engineer Retires After Thirty Years," *Dayton Daily News*, March 1, 1951.

"Olive Dennis Funeral Set," *Baltimore Sun*, November 7, 1957.

"She's Been Working on the Railroad," *Baltimore Sun*, March 13, 1997.

Beischer Harwood, Sharon. "Meet Olive Wetzel Dennis, The Lady Engineer." Presented at the Baltimore Ethical Society, October 26, 2014, Baltimore, MD.

Beischer Harwood, Sharon. "That Lady Engineer: B&O's Olive Dennis Set a Standard," *The Sentinel* 36, No. 3 (2014): 17.

Delich, Helen. "Back-Seat Engineer," *Baltimore Sun*, November 2, 1947.

Dennis, Olive W. "From a Woman's Viewpoint." *Bulletin – American Railway Engineering Association* 43, no. 425 (1941).

Dennis, Olive W. 1928. Dennis Ventilator. United States. US Patent 1693108A, filed December 13, 1927, and issued November 27, 1928.

Dennis, Olive W. Presentation at the Society of Women Engineers at their National Convention, March 6, 1954, Washington, DC.

Giaimo, Cara. "The 'Lady Engineer' Who Took the Pain Out of the Train," *Atlas Obscura*, April 9, 2018.

Gilliland Wright, Mae. "International Women's Day – Women and the Railroads," *National Railroad Hall of Fame*, March 2017.

Hatch, Sybil E. *Changing Our World: True Stories of Women Engineers*. Reston, VA: American Society of Civil Engineers, 2006.

Iowa State University Institute for Transportation. "Women Engineers of the 20th Century: Meet Olive Dennis," *Go! Magazine*, November 10, 2015.

Phillips, Don. "After 158 years, the B. & O. Railroad nears the end of the line." *Washington Post*, November 3, 1986.

Rasmussen, Fred. "She Took the Pain Out of the Train Innovator: One of the First Women to Earn a Cornell Engineering Degree, Olive Dennis Helped Make Rail Travel Less Complicated and More Comfortable." *Baltimore Sun*, November 22, 1997.

Washington Bureau of the Sun. "Miss Olive Dennis to Assist in Determining Railroad Jobs Her Sex Can Be Employed In," *Baltimore Sun*, October 1, 1943.

Wrable, Frank A. "The Royal Blue Line," *The Sentinel* 36, No. 3 (2014): 3.

HORSEDRAWN CAR ·1830·

THE "TOM THUMB" 1830

THE "PHILIP E. THOMAS" 1838

B.A.O.RR

"MOGUL" 600 1875